Freed from Slavery But Still in Bondage

Alice F. Wimberly

ISBN: 978-1-966954-24-8 (paperback)
ISBN: 978-1-966954-25-5 (hardcover)
ISBN: 978-1-966954-26-2 (epub)

Library of Congress Control Number: 2025907732

PREFACT

This is the life of a young black girl born in the South – Evergreen, Alabama, in 1940. Living in a dark era was utter despair even for a child; the black's future did not look very promising. The Southern states were very dominant over people of color; you dared to dream of being better off than your parents were. But unless you had guts, you took what life offered you, powerful voices were not heard in our defence until Martin Luther King came along encouraging people to stand up and not stand down.

Take the initiative in the decisions for your future, including where you want to be educated, this was out of the question until segregation ended. You had no choice on how to pick and choose what you wanted in life. I wanted a successful future, I had a mind to strive and reach my goal.

I began to feel a little ambiguous, after coming out of school and not seeing the resource help that I needed. I got sidetracked, Marriage was my next move, but "I chose the wrong man." Oh, how I wished I had waited and gotten that education first. I thought I was ready to try my wings and, as the old saying goes, "jumped out of the frying pan into the skillet." I realized that I had not separated facts from fantasy and was not rational in my thinking. I woke up to see the real world I found myself living in I faced the tough situation I had gotten myself into. "All those future dreams began to vanish for a moment," because I had refused to see that his goals in life were so different from mine.

And, oh yes! Just plain ignored the visible signs of abuse,

Until moving into an abusive relationship that was awful. My life was in a downward spiral. I had allowed love to cloud my judgment and felt that I could not tell anyone because I had been warned"Watch"

My self-esteem was at an all-time low. I felt like such a big failure and after truly tryingn to make it work, I saw that it was hopeless. Realizing poisoned love will destroy your character and your life will be rendered meaningless. I was determined not to let this happen, I began moving in a positive direction taking control of my life,   turning things around. I pray that those who find themselves in a bad situation can muster the enter strength to move on.

As much as I can remember in the 40s, life was hard. going on into the 50s, it was much harder, because as soon as I was old enough, I was working in the fields and everywhere else. By the time I was ten years old, I could do a woman's job just as well as she could.

My mother and father were God-fearing, churchgoing people, who would beat the devil out of you if you did not do what you were told. We knew how to obey.

They believed in the Scripture that said, "Spare the rod spoil the child.' Well, it worked! It kept us out of trouble, and later on, we all became productive in life. "To all who feel that you were born liberated, read on and you will understand" The battle that was fought for you and I to have the freedom of speech and liberty in America today was won by blood sweat and tears. Unforgettable trail blazers, who trod the path and paid the price in the heat of the day with their blood sweat and tears.

I myself am one of the people who helped pioneer the way so that our children and grandchildren could have a better life. We have come so far in our struggle to be completely liberated and made a lot of progress, and still, there is a long way to go.

Remembering the years, I came up through a life of bondage. I can recall hearing the roosters crow every morning at 4:00 A.M. just like a time clock. Oh, I would have just loved to have wrung their necks, so they could never crow again because that meant soon we would have to crawl out of bed to feed the livestock or whatever needed to be done before the long day began. My father was a sharecropper and poor like all the rest of the black people in the Deep South.

The white people made sure of that. "This time was after slavery had ended." By the way, we had to live, you wouldn't have known it; the farm owners knew that if you ever got your hands on anything, and became successful, you would not need them anymore.

During this era, it was unheard of for a black man or woman to save money. My Grandfather George managed to save a little and, needless to say, they found it and stole all of his life savings; "he went crazy." My parents felt as if there was no hope of freedom. Black people did not use banks because they never had enough to put in them. I guess you could say that they were only people who already had it all. They would let you borrow when it was crop-planting time because they knew most of what you made would belong to them. So we worked hard from sunup to sundown. Every morning before the sun rose, we were in the fields, the ground was wet with dew, and even in the summer, it was cold. Pulling that sack, wet and heavy, filled with cotton, sure was hard.

I can remember the one nice thing about the day that you could not ignore was, no matter how bad you felt, watching the sun as its rays streaked across the horizon, as it began to rise. The robins would begin to sing at the top of the trees as Mother Nature displayed her beauty and nature took its course.

Not long after that, Mom would call out breakfast! We'd all run for the kitchen table, hungry as bears. The temperature was always cold early in the morning and around 10:00 A.M., it would begin to get hot. We went from wet to sweaty. It was very seldom under 90 degrees in the middle of the summer. The only relief from the heat was at the end of the rows where the trees were clustered together. I resented having to work hard just to survive.

Hardship made me become militant. At a very young age, I really was determined to make it in life. "I would not suffer like my parents." My father would work all summer long, from just before daybreak to nightfall, and sometimes he plowed at night by the tractor light. The boss, Mr. Hormel, his field had to be plowed first. We worked in our field when the opportunity arose.

My parents used to say "There
is no rest for the weary." I knew then that I had to
do something to escape that awful life, but what?
Sometimes after Dad had gathered his crop, and
the loans were paid off, there was barely enough
money to buy shoes for all of the children. Never
had enough, we just got by. We got one pair of shoes
and they had better last you for the year. If our shoes
wore out on the bottom, we would wear the top. I
knew I would not live in poverty, forever, and I
knew this was not the way life was intended to be.
At this time a new era was beginning; there had to
be some changes. I was not going to live in a house
that leaked so badly until you had to get out the pans
to set them around to catch the water or shove the
bed to the middle of the floor, just so you wouldn't
get rained on. It was so cold in the houses in those
days that we slept in between the mattresses to keep
warm.

I dreamed of the day I could buy the house of my choice, in any community I wanted. I knew that there were many mountains to climb before we as a race could come to that.

By now I was coming out of grade school, just making it, Going to school on a part-time basis. We had to stay in the fields for most of the school season. It's a wonder I made it. We'd stay up late studying by the old lantern light when we could go to school. I always imagined myself being somebody. My imaginary friend and I were always going to marry a tall, dark, and handsome man. Life was really a dream at that time, and I knew that somehow, someday, it would be a reality.

One day all my dreams would come true because I was going to do whatever it took to make it happen. In school, we participated in saying the Pledge of Allegiance to the flag of the United States of America every day.

It was supposed to be with liberty and justice for all.

The "big lie!" We finally got justice, but we had to become militant. Stand up and be counted and fight for what was supposed to be ours already. It was just a figment of the imagination at that time. Our school was a big, old-fashioned open building, heated with an old pot-bellied heater, which smelled of coal, but we were glad to be there, getting away from home. The fact that I would have to work in other people's homes, I was glad to go to school. Mrs. Brooks was Mr. Hormel's wife. We lived in their place. My dad worked the farm and we cleaned the house. That was the deal.

I guess that was in exchange for rent.

If you worked and ran everything right, you were a "good old Nigger." It seems I would always be the one chosen to go and work. I always did a good job and was a good worker. Most of the husband's workers were animals. I had to fight to keep from being raped on a daily basis. I guess my job included pushing and shoveing, because I sure had to do some. Every time Mr. Hormel's wife would leave or just be out of sight, Mr. Hormel would sneak up from behind, wrap his hands around my breast, or try to hustle me down on the bed Boy, the fight was on! He didn't like it, but he didn't dare say anything because he knew if his wife found out he was touching a "Nigger gal," he would be in trouble. I hated him and dreaded when I had to go over there to work. I will never forget the day when Mom was called to work as well, and he, Mr. Hormel, grabbed her around her breast, but she gave him a shove across the kitchen floor. The floor was extremely slick because it was freshly waxed,
and boy, he hit it.

When Mrs. Brooks returned from the market, he was clutching his chest and breathing hard, but I bet he never told her what really happened. Mrs. Brooks took him to the hospital and he was admitted. The next day she went to visit, She said to my mom, "Sue, come on and go with me to visit Mr. Hormel. I know you want to see him." Reluctantly, she agreed, for there was no graceful way out. She was scared to death for pushing him down in the first place. She knew that he could have told a different story and there she would have been without a leg to stand on. They made their way to the hospital, and Mrs. Brooks left something in the car, so she said, "Sue, stay here and take care of Hormel." My mother nodded her head. When Mrs. Brooks left the room, Mr. Hormel rose up off the bed and whispered as low as he could, "You old devil!" Mother never said a word, and neither did her facial expression change. In those days if a white man killed a black man, he was never convicted, but if Freed from Slavery but Still in Bondage

The roles were reversed, the black man was sentenced to the electric chair, if the mob didn't get him first. The words of "liberty and justice for all" stuck in my mind. We had neither. My oldest sister Novella would tell me some of the horrible things that really happened. Perhaps I was too young to remember every detail and some I chose to forget. My dad finally got a pretty decent car; it was a green '49 Chevy. "I thought we were really somebody now." One day while driving from town, he came up behind a white lady. She was driving really slow, so he waited until he could pass and drove around her, never thinking anything about it. She went home and told a lie to her husband that he tried to run her off the road. Around 12:00 o'clock midnight, the KKK came to our home, and kicked the door in, and dragged my dad outside.

The roles were reversed, the black man was sentenced to the electric chair, if the mob didn't get him first. The words of "liberty and justice for all" stuck in my mind. We had neither. My oldest sister Novella would tell me some of the horrible things that really happened. Perhaps I was too young to remember every detail and some I chose to forget.

My dad finally got a pretty decent car; it was a green '49 Chevy. "I thought we were really somebody now." One day while driving from town, he came up behind a white lady. She was driving really slow, so he waited until he could pass and drove around her, never thinking anything about it. She went home and told a lie to her husband that he tried to run her off the road. Around 12:00 o'clock midnight, the KKK came to our home, and kicked the door in, and dragged my dad outside.

would have gone hungry. So all the white people were not bad. Even back then, those people were loving and caring. They would help you undercover, fearing what the neighbors would say.

My Aunt Pete became a mistress to one of the big men in the community not willingly but by force. There was nothing she could do but cry and do what he wanted.

Slavery was over on paper only; "she was his sex slave," unwilling and scared. I guess he must have really fallen in love with her later on. Apparently, he was concerned about his name because he wouldn't touch her in public. No one was supposed to touch a black person in that way. Somehow his wife and children knew about it, and they hated her. They were afraid of him as well, so they kept quiet and did nothing. He was a powerful man, so that saved her neck.

I am sure his wife thought Aunt Pete wanted that,

but she had to do what he wanted or he'd beat her. She

ran away many times only to be found by him wherever

she went. He could not scare her into not leaving, so he

would say to her. "Stop acting like a fool, running away,

you can't hide from me." He promised her a beauty

shop,

knowing her dream was to become a beautician, to be

a career woman, and to have her own business. I

suppose

Aunt Pete had more guts than the rest. She set her eyes

on

having a life of her own, not having to be told when and

where not to go. Mr. Armour, somehow, always knew

when she left home; he watched her like a hawk.

Freed from Slavery but Still in Bondage

One night, she wanted to go to a party really bad,

with her classmates, but she knew he would not approve

of it, for fear that someone else may take interest. Mr.

Armour must have been watching the house. That night

she slipped off, or at least she thought she did. When

the party was over, she came home to find him waiting

in the bushes for her return. He pulled her out and beat

her within inches of her life, and then he doctored her

back to health. She was not able to walk for three days.

Her mother knew what happened, but she was too

afraid

to do anything about it. All she could do was sit there,

rocking, and crying. Lizzy, who was my grandmother,

was alone. My grandfather had died and left her with

five

children and no one to stand up for them, so they took

whatever was dished out to them.

At that point,

I understood why Mother was so afraid when she pushed Mr. Hormel. You just didn't cross white folks. She'd sit and talk for hours telling me all those things and tears would fill her eyes. There were boundaries you did not dare cross and colored mixing was one, but somehow, all those half-white babies would appear.

You never knew who their daddies were unless
they looked so much like their dads, and pretty soon
mom and child would disappear. I was told they would
send them away once a baby came. As time went on, my
aunt made up her mind she was leaving; she decided
that she was either going to be free or die trying.
She knew that she would have to go farther than she
had gone before if she was going to get away.

Alice Faye Wimberly Leaving without being seen was the dilemma. By this time they knew something had to be done. My dad, her brother–in–law, put a plan in action; it had to look as if nothing was going on. where there is a will to be persistent, there's a way." The plan was to put her in the same scheme To help her escape!

Remember, "where there's big box that they took hogs to the market in. It worked, although she and the rest were scared silly. She rode right past his house with what few clothes she had in the box on the back of a truck. Well, they took her to the bus station where she began her journey to freedom. I had run away from a bad situation and thought I had it hard until I heard of the hard life she had.

It's funny because I always thought moving to the city would be the answer. After spending a short time with my Aunt Pete, I realized that prejudice was everywhere and unless you made a difference in your life, you would always be the underdog. My mom's sister, Aunt Pete, came to visit. I told her what I had encountered when I had to clean the boss's house, thinking I had gone through something, but after she told me what she went through, I was considered blessed. I wanted to get even with them but didn't have a leg to stand on.

Aunt Pete had become the mistress of a well-known man, who made house calls to check on his people. Most of the time for the wrong reason, Mr. Armour, would come and take her to the woods, whenever he pleased.

After going into the big city and seeing a different side of life, She took control of her life and began the long journey to freedom, conquering her low self-esteem, realizing self-worth, and just letting go of the past. Refusing to let go of the past held her hostage. It overpowered you, defeating your purpose in life. Remembering the bad side of life should serve one purpose only and that is to let Someone else knows, that no matter what you go through, you can overcome it.

She took the courage, to run again from the same man who had found and beat her. So for a while, she lived in bondage. She was putting distance between the past and the future, and that is just what I was trying to do, find freedom that's felt as well as seen.

Maybe all of her redemption didn't come right then, but she was headed in the right direction. "One must restore faith in humanity" when your dignity has been scarred. "That was hard for her to do." As it turned out, he did try to find her, but in a city as big as Miami, it

was hard to locate someone when you didn't know where

to look. She hid for a long time, and one day she was walking down the street; someone dropped some keys

After going into the big city and seeing a different side of life,

she took control over her life and began the long journey to freedom, conquering her low self-esteem, realizing self-worth, and just letting go of the past. Refusing to let go of the past held her hostage. It overpowered you, defeating your purpose in life. Remembering the bad side of life should serve one purpose only and that is to let someone else know, that no matter what you go through, you can overcome it.

She took the courage, to run again from the same man who had found and beat her. So for a while, she lived in bondage. She was putting distance between the past and the future, and that is just what I was trying to do, find freedom that's felt as well as seen.

Maybe all of her redemption didn't come right then, but she was headed in the right direction. "One must restore faith in humanity" when your dignity has been scarred.

"That was hard for her to do." As it turned out, he did try to find her, but in a city as big as Miami, it was hard to locate someone when you didn't know where to look. She hid for a long time, and one day she was walking down the street; when someone dropped some keys.

The sound of the keys falling to the ground made her turn and look, and there he was. It just so happened she saw him before he saw her.
I was a young lady by this time in my early teens, and she was in her late thirties. By then things had already begun to change. I could push, shove, and say

No, if I wanted to, I now had that choice. She became the beautician she wanted to be and had a very successful business. Many people looked up to her for the graceful way she lived her life. She should have made world history. Like all the rest of us, she had to fight to get there, but she made it. God bless her soul, she departed this life in November 2002. "She leaves the legacy of hope and courage."

After all our long talks, I was more sure than ever that I was going to make it, over the obstacles and life's mountains that I knew I would have to climb, being poor. She taught me enough to know, if you fall, just try it again; quitters never succeed, and those who succeed never quit.

After I made it through elementary school, I went to live with Aunt Pete in Miami. This was one of the best things that could have happened to me, at least I didn't have to watch the school bus loaded with the kids in the afternoon, ride by coming from the school. You could hear that long old yellow school bus, A mile away the kids would peer out of the window, as they rode by, and we would be bent over pulling that sack of cotton, hot and tired. It was all I could do not cry because I wanted to go

to school like they did. Sometimes, it would be some of the crops we were harvesting. When it rained, we were so glad, because it was too wet to work, so we prayed it would rain. Wednesday was the day I hated because it was my day to work in that house that I hated so much.

After I told my aunt what was happening, she and I made plans, to help me run away like she did, me from one problem: and she from another. I was so glad to be able to go to school every day. I was far behind my classmates because I'd hardly gone to school. Waking up not having to go to the cow pen or cotton patch, was a real joy. Aunt Pete took me away from those horrible conditions and gave me a chance to learn. I always wanted to go to college and teach school someday. But I didn't keep my eyes on my goals and marriage overwhelmed me until Bound by the Color of Your Skin searching for equality liberty, and justice was anything but easy. Your life could not mean more than your freedom; be free or live in bondage. The powerful white man in the South knew he was losing control of the younger black men and women. Then the KKK began to burn crosses in people's yards, letting them know who was in authority.

The long white robe and white hood were supposed to put you back in your place, to put some fear in you. Men like Dr. Martin Luther King rose up in the face of adversity. He did not mind dying to see all men have a better quality of life. It was not always that you could go into any restaurant, and sit anywhere and eat. That privilege was won by the protest marches, boycotts, and sit-ins "and yes, some bloodshed."

Lula Nettles was one of those who risked her life in places where black people are forbidden to go!

"In Selma, Alabama, the NAACP emerged." The committee would take a position in places where the law was not upheld. They demanded to be served peacefully. They were not denied but charged $15 for a hamburger, which should only cost 35 cents. They did not eat it; it was just time to demand to be served anywhere and in any restaurant they chose. Every one of them was shaking in their boots.

There is no telling what those hamburgers had in them! Just getting served was a breaking point. Negroes were allowed to go to the back door to buy what they wanted, but they couldn't go in. As long as you got wanted and left it was fine, but we were not good enough to go in. All that would have to change.

God had sent a man like Moses to lead his people out of bondage, knowing that somewhere down in the line, it would cost him his life. The freedom we enjoy today began when he was kicked and thrown in jail, tear-gassed, and water-hosed down. Having done all to stand, he stood anyhow, saying in his spirit, things had to change. Many great men and women of the days of old somehow have overcome the things I have had to come across. Maybe in a different way, but with the same meaning. God created all men equal. If this was so, where was the equality? He knew it had to be won. Our foundation was shaky because knowledge had been hidden from the black man. Many were unlearned in school because we were not exposed to the learning materials that the next schools had.

It had to begin with the school, in the curriculum, but that was not about to change without integration. Again there were more blood baths. After we won the right for integration all of the schools had to be brought up to code. I can remember thinking that I was on my way. Soon reality set in and I began to realize that I was only halfway. They would send white teachers to teach, but no white students participated. They wanted to look like they were complying with the law. My dad would say

"Girl, learn all you can 'cause if you don't know, you may never!" NAACP saw right through the false attempt and the staged boycotts and marches. Then the busing law was passed, putting a handful of black kids in the white school. I wasn't fortunate to be one.

By the time I was out of school, the only experience I had was cleaning other people's houses. I had no money, but I yearned to learn.

I knew in my heart that one day I would find a way to succeed. The education that I obtained by going to school was just enough for the basic skills of life. Even though all the changes were made after I got out of school, it was better for my children. We should not take it lightly or forget so that we never become ungrateful for the price that was paid for our freedom and having the ability to do with ourlives as we please. If you want to own an airplane and fly over towns at Christmastime, as my sister Novella always wanted to be able to do, Just go ahead and begin your dreams. It won't come to you by sitting and holding your hands. Why did she feel like that Mom and Dad were not able to do for us kids? The money just was not there was always a house full of kids. Sometimes the homeless live there too. Mother had a kind heart and she would reach out to anyone in need of a place to lay his or her head and a home-cooked meal. Somehow through the sharing by our parents and what little we had, we survived.

Once a year at Christmastime, we knew that we would get some goodies. The old folks would magnif The old folks would magnify

Christmas and we couldn't wait. One year would feel as if it was two years in the waiting process. Mom would say, "You better be good or Santa won't come to visit." As the year progressed, in the back of my mind, I wouldn't lose sight of that, if I wasn't good, I would not receive my gift. "Great motivation, huh?" Finally, Christmas Eve arrived and everyone was anxiously awaiting bedtime.

Dad would say, "All right, youngin's, it's time for bed." We would race to get in the bed in front of the old fireplace. Jumping in and covering our heads tightly to make it dark, we were sure to go straight to sleep. The next morning we would jump out of bed to grab our sacks full of goodies.

We were so happy. An apple, three oranges, some raisins, nuts, and one peppermint stick. You would have thought we got what our hearts had desired, running outside to show the other neighborhood children our Freed from Slavery but Still in Bondage gifts. I will never forget the feeling I had when I realized that we were poor.

Opening up my bag to show my gifts,
they laughed and made fun of us. The other little girls had baby dolls and tea sets. I hung my head and walked back to the house, thinking that life wasn't fair, but one day I would be able to give my children a better life, and we wouldn't have to live in a house with holes in the floors or in the ceilings. Our parents knew how we felt but could do nothing about the situation we were in. I believe that's why my sister Novella has such a big heart. In so many ways, she carried on Mom and Dad's tradition.

She has been a great asset to the community

of Mobile, Alabama. She is and has always been a foster

parent for many lost children, giving them things that

she could never get as a child.

Many children today get what their heart desire,

and some parents never mention how they reached this

place in their lives, to have the finances to do what they

please and work on the jobs they desire. They do those

who suffered for our freedom a great injustice, when we

fail to educate the younger generation about the great price

that was paid to get there.

When I stand in my kitchen at the sink and run water from the faucet, a part of me still says I am grateful because our people no longer have to go down to the spring and carry buckets of water.These were wide-open, dug-out places in the ground: sometimes when looking down into it, we saw creatures crawling around at the bottom of it. We would dip it out it out and keep on going.

The white people had running water because they could buy electric pumps. A few years later water lines were run through the neighborhood where black peiople lived. "Even that had to be fought for," before they would bring lines into the poor folks' community. So there was a time longer when we would bring all of our water from the spring to wash. It would take a lot of water to wash for all of us. Most of the washing would take a lot of water to wash for. Most of the washing would be done at night because we worked all day.

If you were tired, it was too bad. The washing had to be done so that we would have clean clothes. "Hot baths were lavishing." We'd set those big washtubs full of water in the sun in the morning, and by night the water would be plenty warm.

The day I got a house with a bathroom and running water was pure heaven. As I look back over my life, and see where I am today, I am grateful, and never will I forget the sacrifice made for me to get up and be what I want to be today. The choice was not given by desire but through sacrifice. We all knew it was not always going to be easy to be successful and live an accomplished life.